Sergiev Posad

Sergiev Posad

Museum-Reserve

English Edition

If you have several days left at your disposal after having done the main sights of Moscow, you will certainly be offered a trip to the Trinity-Sergius Laura. Accept without any hesitation. Transportation is laborious. Yet no one has ever regretted the experience.

THÉOPHILE GAUTIER, *A Journey to Russia,* Paris 1867

ART–RODNIK • *Moscow* • *1997*

Texts and selection:
T.N.MANUSHINA
S.V.NIKOLAYEVA
O.I.ZARITSKAYA

Layout, design, typesetting:
L.V.DENISENKO
V.Ya.CHERNIYEVSKY

Translation from the Russian:
N.A.BELYAKOVA

Photography:
Yu.V. ARTAMONOV, V.Ye. GIPPENREITER,
V.N. KORNYUSHIN, V.V. MITIN, V.A. POLYAKOV,
N.N. RAKHMANOV, N.N. SOLOVIOV,
V.Ya. ZAGUMENNOV

Sergiev Posad
History and Art

S ome Russian towns are so attractive and original that, having visited them once, you will always remember them and, probably, feel like coming back again and again. Sergiev Posad in Moscow Region with its ancient history and picturesque scenery is certainly one of them. One can vividly feel links with the past here; a native seems to get in touch with his historic and spiritual roots, and a foreign visitor can unveil mysteries of Russian world view.

The town of painters, wood-carvers, toy-makers developed from the villages and settlements surrounding the Trinity-St. Sergius Laura — one of the ancient and most revered Russian monasteries, a historic centre of Russian Orthodox (16).

Father Superior Sergius of Radonezh and Foundation of the Trinity Monastery

The Trinity Monastery was founded in the mid-14th century by "The greatest saint of Old Russia", Venerable Sergius of Radonezh, who became a symbol of consolidation and revival of the Russian state (1*). According to *The Life of St. Sergius*, compiled by the founder's younger contemporary Epiphanius the Wise, Sergius (Bartholomew before taking monastic vows) was a son of Boyar Kirill of Rostov, who moved with his family to Radonezh, a centre of a small apanage principality upon Moscow Prince's patronage. As a youth Bartholomew was attracted by a life of a hermit, but at his parents' request he had to postpone consecration and took monastic vows only after their death. Having buried their parents in the Khotkovo Monastery, Bartholomew and his brother Stephen, who had already taken monastic vows, left for the woods in the vicinity of Radonezh and found a place for a hermitage 15 kilometres from the town.

On the top of a high hill, surrounded by the Konchura River, the brothers built a small church and a cell (2). Stephen could not bear toilsome ascetic life

* Numbers given refer to illustrations.

and went to the Moscow Epiphany Monastery, leaving his brother, who had been ordained monk and received the name of Sergius by that time, in seclusion (3). Yet, in a year other monks, looking for solitude, began to join him. The author of *The Life of St. Sergius*, besides the difficulties and asceticism of the brethren's life, described the miracles and prediction, promising to turn the modest abode, where "simple poverty was a source of treasures", into the most prosperous and famous Russian monastery – the Trinity-St. Sergius Laura. A lot of painted and carved icons depict *The Appearance of the Virgin to St. Sergius of Radonezh* described in *The Life*, when the Virgin promised to protect this abode for ever (60). In the works of art of the subsequent period a scene of the Vision of Birds (8) was often depicted, as if to throw away the doubts of Sergius striving for a quiet life of a hermit and displeased with the growing number of monks. The Virgin sent him the vision of many birds as a symbol of his numerous disciples and successors.

Sergius of Radonezh is one of the most outstanding characters in Russian history. A hermit, who abandoned the world for the sake of inner self-discipline, he had to take an active part in the policy of unification led by Moscow Princes: he was sent to Nizhny Novgorod to persuade Prince Boris to recognize the priority of his brother Prince Dmitry of Suzdal; he managed to bring Prince Oleg of Ryazan to peace and union with Moscow. The very dedication of his monastery to the Trinity, symbolizing universal love and unity corresponded to the hopes of people tired of apanage conflicts. Sergius of Radonezh belonged to the generation, which was brought up when Russia suffered from the Tartar opression, that had during more than a hundred years, and was regarded as an inevitable heavenly punishment. However, Sergius became an energetic advocate of young Moscow Prince Dmitry Ivanovich, a representative of a younger generation, which had courage to face the invaders in battle, and attacked the enemies with "the invincible wall, burying them under the bones of many thousands of warriors" at Kulikovo Field in 1380. Sergius had given his blessing to Prince Dmitry before the great battle, foretelling the victory and inspiring Russian people with "courage and spirits" (V.O. Klyuchevsky). The chronicles also record that Sergius sent with the army two monks, "experienced warriors", Peresvet and Oslyabya. According to the legend, the Battle of Kulikovo started with a single combat of Peresvet with a Tartar warrior Temir-Murza.

Sergius did not wish to attract attention to his personality (at first he even refused to become Father Superior of his monastery; he did not want to be ordained Metropolitan), but he became well-known in Russia and, probably abroad, in his lifetime. There is a legend narrating about Patriarch Philotheus of Constantinople giving his blessing to Sergius for the introduction of the rules of a cenobitic monastery (the new rules for the 14th-century Russian convents, determining common church services and belongings, strict discipline and subordination to the Father Superior). The 14th-century gold cross (4,5) was kept in the Monastery as a symbol of this blessing.

Sergius, strictly fulfilling his Christian and monastic duty, became an outstanding symbol of Russian spirit and patriotism for his contemporaries and for all following generations.

According to the Russian historian V.O. Klyuchevsky, Venerable Sergius of Radonezh was one of those people, who personified and consolidated the moral

1. *St. Sergius of Radonezh*
Mounted icon
16th century
Trinity-St. Sergius Monastery (?)
Donated by Boyar Vasily Konstantinovich Velyaminov
Tempera on panel, silver, embossing, gilding;
30 x 23 *

* All measurements are given in centimetres, height before width.

forces of the great nation, damaged by severe oppression, and who took the nation, which had temporarily lost its way, back to its straight historic road.

The authority of Sergius and faith in his special protection insured glory and fame for his monastery. The Trinity monks founded a lot of cloisters, that were organizationally and spiritually attached to the Trinity Monastery. After Sergius's death and canonization, which took place in 1422, these cloisters contributed to the development of St. Sergius's cult, as well as to the promotion of the policy of Moscow's Grand Princes in all Russian lands.

The Trinity-St. Sergius Monastery in the 15th-16th Centuries

We can just imagine how the Trinity Monastery looked like in the past. Time and fire did not give us a chance to see its wooden structures. In 1408, the monastery was burnt down during the siege of Tartar Khan Edigei. The monks with the Superior Nikon, a disciple and successor to Sergius of Radonezh managed to escape in the woods. They returned several years later, and the monastery was reconstructed.

Father Superior Nikon with the support of Moscow Princes laid the foundation of economic and political status of the Trinity-St. Sergius Monastery (10,11).

At Sergius's time the Trinity Monastery received first donations and privileges from Grand Princes, and since the 15th century regular donations in money, land and treasures came from representatives of different strata of the society. A legend tells that with the funds given by Dmitry Donskoi's son Yuri, Prince of Zvenigorod, a godson of Sergius, the white-stone Cathedral of the Trinity (19) was constructed.

2. Construction
of the monastery
in the 14th century
Copy of a miniature
from the Life of St. Sergius
of Radonezh
16th century

2

It is the oldest surviving monument in the monastery architectural ensemble. Built in 1422 "in praise" of Venerable Sergius of Radonezh, it became one of the first Russian memorials. The Old Russian masons constructed the austere, laconic and modestly decorated cathedral. This small, yet majestic uprising cathedral, created in traditions of Early Moscow architecture, corresponded to Sergius's severe time, with his asceticism and his elevated idea of unity and universal love, which he dedicated to his monastery (20). In ancient times, when the entrance was from the West, the Cathedral of the Trinity met a pilgrim at the gate, like Superior Sergius himself. Now we enter the monastery from the opposite eastern side, and it seems significant that our road to the cathedral passes along its entire territory, like through its history, through all those five centuries, marked by magnificent buildings in its architectural ensemble.

The interior of the cathedral was decorated by a group of artists headed by the celebrated icon painters Daniel Chorny and Andrei Rublev. Unfortunately, the frescoes have not survived, being repainted in the 17th century. But the iconostasis is still decorated with forty 15th-century icons (22). For this cathedral Andrei

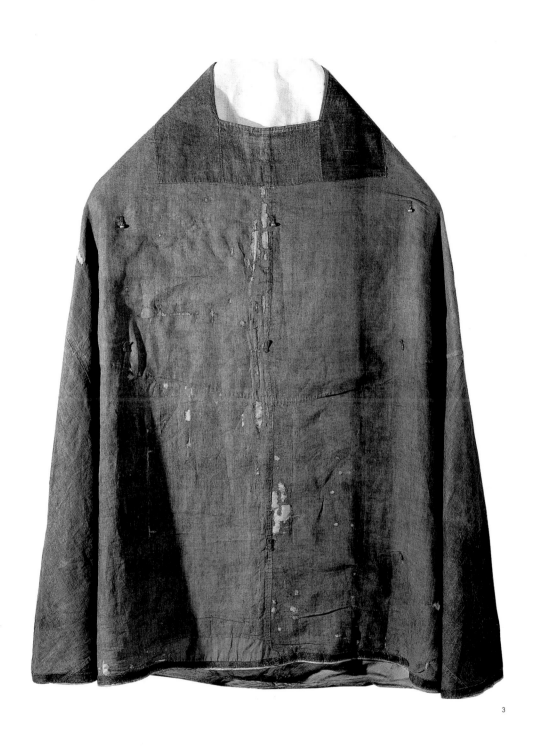

3

3. *Phelonion of Superior Sergius of Radonezh*

14th century

Linen, damask; length, 141

Rublev painted his world-famous icon *The Old Testament Trinity*, which became a symbol of Old Russian culture. (Since 1929, the icon has been displayed in the Moscow Tretyakov Gallery.) The Royal Doors of the iconostasis are mounted in chased silvergilt frame, donated to the monastery by Tsar Mikhail Feodorovich Romanov. The cathedral contains the relics of St. Sergius of Radonezh. They are preserved in a chased silver shrine, made in the 16th century by silversmiths of the Armoury Chamber in Moscow Kremlin to Ivan the Terrible's order. Above the shrine is a silver canopy donated in the 18th century by Empress Anna Ioannovna (23). In the Cathedral of the Trinity Moscow Grand Princes and Russian Tsars baptized their sons, here they came for blessing before or after important events in social and private life.

In the 15th century, during the cruel feudal war for the royal throne, Moscow Grand Prince Vasily II, a grandson of Prince Dmitry, was captured here. Despite the attempts of the monastery to settle the conflict between the descendants of Dmitry Donskoi, he was returned to Moscow blinded and nicknamed the Dark.

The church, constructed in 1548 over the tomb of Superior Nikon of Radonezh (21), is attached to the southern part of the cathedral. So, his spiritual link with the monastery founder, Sergius of Radonezh

4

5

4, 5. *Cross-reliquary*

(obverse and reverse)

14th century

Presented to Superior

Sergius by Patriarch

Philotheus of Constantinople

Gold, engraving;

4 x 2.6

was stressed in architecture. This idea of unity and succession was subsequently reflected in pictorial and applied arts: icon-painting, embroidery, 18th-century engraving.

By the late 15th century the unification of the Russian principalities had yielded results in politics and economy, as well as in the evolution of culture. Moscow absorbed and developed the best achievements of different centres. So, it seems only natural that the craftsmen from distant Pskov were commissioned to construct a new belfry in the Monastery of St. Sergius, who was a great supporter of consolidation. In 1476, they built the small Church of the Holy Ghost with the bells at the base of the cupola (24). This type of structure was widespread in Pskov, but quite new in Moscow. Even the bells were rung in the Pskovian manner. The bell, fixed on the movable beam, was swung with a long rope. However, the masons from Pskov did not simply reproduce the familiar type: they combined constructive originality of Pskov with characteristic forms and decoration of Moscow architecture. Thus, the creation of Pskov craftsmen was harmoniously placed near the Cathedral of the Trinity, an example of Early Moscow architecture, stressing again common traditions in Russian art. For a long time the belfry of the Church

6. *St. Nicholas*

Icon. 14th century. Rostov

According to legend, the icon was in Sergius's cell

Tempera on panel; 49 x 36

7. *The Virgin Hodegetria*

Icon, 14th century. Mounting, 16th century. Moscow

According to legend, the icon was in Sergius's cell

Tempera on panel; silver, pearls, precious stones; embossing,

filigree, gilding, stringing; 47 x 38

of the Holy Ghost served as a watch-tower. In this quiet and cosy church Ivan the Terrible prayed after the death of his son Ivan, whom he had murdered in a fit of anger. He confessed his secret only to several people, including Father Superior and Cellarer of the Trinity Monastery.

Ivan the Terrible's attitude towards the Trinity-St. Sergius Monastery, like his attitude towards the Church in general, was complicated and contradictory. The Tsar reproached the monks with breaking the monastic rules, made attempts to restrict the monasteries' land property; among the tortured and executed in the "oprichnina capital" Alexandrova Sloboda (situated several kilometres from the Trinity-St. Sergius Monastery) there was a Trinity monk, hunted down by bears. At the Tsar's will, disagreable boyars were made to take vows in the monastery. At the same time, Ivan the Terrible frequently visited the Trinity-St. Sergius Monastery and donated numerous treasures; in his reign the Trinity hegumens were ordained the title of Archimandrite, which was the "highest for all monasteries".

8. *The Vision of Birds to St. Sergius.*
By Mikhail Gadalov
after I.S. Boldyrev's drawing
1859.
The Trinity-St. Sergius Laura
Lithograph tinted
with water-colours;
39 x 45

By the order of Ivan the Terrible and with his donations, the largest five-domed Cathedral of the Dormition was constructed (1559-1585) (25). The Tsar and his family were present for its foundation. Nearly all Russian monasteries had cathedrals dedicated to the Virgin revered as patroness of Rus. The cathedral in the Trinity Monastery was dedicated to the Dormition of the Virgin. The victory over the Khanates of Kazan and Astrakhan was, presumably, the reason for its construction. In 1552, before his campaign, Ivan the Terrible visited the monastery and attended the service. In 1556, the Tsar received here a message about the capture of Astrakhan (Ivan the Terrible might have ordered to plate with gold the cupola of the Trinity Cathedral in memory of that event). The Cathedral of the Dormition, austere and majestic, occupied the central part of the monastery, after the wooden cells had been moved to the fortress wall. The Cathedral of the Dormition in the Moscow Kremlin was used as its prototype. But, in contrast with the white-stone Kremlin cathedral, the cathedral in the monastery was built of brick; it is larger in size, its walls are more massive, but their decorative band is more simple.

The construction was delayed, as Ivan the Terrible lost interest in his idea and stopped providing money for its realization. The devastating fire of 1567 slackened the pace of its construction too. The cathedral was consecrated after Ivan the Terrible's death. It was painted only in 1684. Thirty-five icon painters, whose names are recorded in the " chronicle" in the lower part of the wall, within sur-

prisingly short period of a hundred summer days, created polychrome frescoes, covering with them the large surface inside the cathedral (26). Dmitry and Vasily Grigoriev are mentioned the first among the painters. The beautiful frescoes coming down to us, are in perfect harmony with magnificent gilt woodcarving of the impressively large iconostasis. The icons in the Cathedral of the Dormition are referred to the 16th and 17th century. The interior is decorated with two cast and chased bronze church chandeliers skilfully made in the 17th century in the Moscow Armoury.

The onion-shaped cupolas and bright exterior decoration date back to the 18th century, like the parvises – porches, attached to the northern and southern façades, and the intricate portal which replaced the vaulted parvis.

The Heroic Defence of the Monastery in 1608-1609

By the mid-16th century, when Moscow was surrounded by a ring of fortress-towns, the Trinity-St. Sergius Monastery had become a stronghold, protecting the north-eastern approaches to the capital. The wooden fence was replaced by a stone wall with 12 towers (17). At that time the fortress was not high, but it was well equipped. The walls were 6 metres high and about 3 metres wide. The towers permitted to fire at the area right beneath the walls. Ivan the Terrible controlled the fortification himself. He released from the state duties the monastery peasant builders, gave a privilege to the monastery authorities to take stone in any region free of charge and taxes, and donated three thousand roubles.

Half a century later the fortress wall withstood the artillery fire during the siege of the Polish-Lithuanian invaders that lasted for 16 months. The defence of the Trinity-St. Sergius Monastery in the early 17th century was one of the most heroic episodes in Russian history. When the Polish-Lithuanian troops of False Dmitry II approached Moscow and his commanders Hetman Sapieha and Lisowski captured Pereslavl-Zalessky, Rostov, Suzdal and other towns to the northeast from the capital, the Trinity-St. Sergius Monastery found itself in complete isolation. The rumours of the monastery treasures attracted the invaders, who

10

10. *Phelonion of Superior Nikon of Radonezh*
Early 15th century
Damask, taffeta, linen, brocade;
126 x 216

9. *St. Nikon of Radonezh*
Pall. Detail
16th century. Moscow
Damask, coloured silks,
silver and gold thread;
embroidery; length, 94

expected an easy victory. Heinrich Staden, a German in oprichnina of Ivan the Terrible, had also tempted his fellow-countrymen with a prospect to conquer "the richest monastery all over the country" by a detachment of a thousand men " half mounted, half on foot". But the invaders did not take into consideration just one thing – courage and determination of the fortress defenders. They boldly corrected the estimations of the adventurers, like Staden, and predetermined a completely different result of the campaign.

The inhabitants of villages and settlements around the monastery burnt their houses and took refuge behind the monastery walls. About three thousand defenders, including the detachment of 500 warriors brought from Moscow by A.I. Golokhvastov and G.B. Dolgorukov-Roshcha, resisted the Polish-Lithuanian army numbering 30 thousand. Nevertheless, no assault was a success, in vain did the invaders try to climb the walls of the fortress, which they contemptuously called a "bast-basket". Having failed to attack the fortress, the invaders resorted to cunning–they planned to sap one of the towers, blast it and burst into the monastery through the gap. The defenders knew about the sap and realized the threat, but they could not discover it for a long time. The sap was located, when it was nearly ready and filled with powder. It was under the strong Pyatnitskaya Tower in the south-eastern corner. A group of the defenders sallied the enemies at the entrance. Two peasants Nikon Shilov and Pyotr Slota of the neighbouring village of Klementyevo blew up the sap, sacrificing their lives. Another monastery detachment, taking advantage of the enemy's confusion, attacked the batteries, firing the monastery from the west, and captured "the whole detail". But more ordeals were in store for the defenders: severe winter cold, starvation and epidemics, which caused more losses than military actions. Tsar Boris Godunov's daughter Xenia, staying in the monastery at that time, wrote: "...everyday they bury twenty people and more, and those people who...walk, they do not control themselves, they all have lost the use of their legs...". The Cellarer of the Trinity-St. Sergius Monastery Avraamy Palitsyn, author of *The Tale of the Siege* thought that in winter 2,125 people, not mentioning women and children, were killed or died of "illneses caused by the siege".

11

11. *Panagia*

First quarter 15th century

Moscow

Once worn by Superior Nikon

Silver; casting, engraving,

gilding;

13.3 x 9.5

The invaders expected the defenders to be broken by the severe circumstances, so they undertook three attacks in spring and summer of 1609. But the fortress resisted them and withstood another half a year till the troops of M. V. Skopin-Shuisky came. On January 12 of 1610, after the decisive battle by the monastery wall Sapieha and Lisowski raised the siege withdrawing to Dmitrov.

As history willed, the war with Poland that lasted for more than 10 years came to end here, not far from the monastery. In 1618, in the monastery-ruled

12

12. *Trinity-St. Sergius Monastery*

Icon. 17th century

Tempera on panel; 44.5 x 36.5

village of Deulino the Moscow ambassadors, headed by Boyar F. Sheremetev, signed the armistice between Russia and Poland.

The heroic defence of the Trinity-St. Sergius Monastery set an example, inspiring Russian people for the struggle with the invaders. Patriotism, determination and strong spirit were again associated with the Trinity-St. Sergius Monastery in people's opinion. No wonder, all Russian Tsars came on pilgrimage to this monastery before and after their military campaigns, and the warriors took icons with the image of St. Sergius with them..

13. *The Trinity-St. Sergius Laura*
as seen from the south-east
Mid-19th century
By Louis Pierre Alfonse Bichebois
J.-P. Lemercie's lithographic printing-office, Paris
Black-and-white lithograph. 30x40

The Trinity-St. Sergius Monastery in the 17th Century

For all misfortunes of the Time of Troubles, the Trinity-St. Sergius Monastery quickly healed the "martial wounds" with the help of numerous donations. The neighbouring settlements were rebuilt. The walls were reconstructed, their width and length were nearly doubled, more cannons were installed. Yet the fortress was never used for defence again. In the 17th – 19th century, the towers were reconstructed, their tops and decorations were changed. The Duck Tower in the north-eastern corner is exceptionally beautiful, it is crowned with a stone sculpture of a duck (28). The names of Beer, Granary, Water and Cellarer Towers prove their household function.

The wooden monastic cells within the walls were rebuilt in stone. The infirmary with the Church of SS. Zosima and Savvaty were a kind of memorial to the fortress defenders (27). It is an original combination of the civic structure (hospital for old and sick monks) and the church which seems to grow up from the ground floor of the infirmary. The Church of SS. Zosima and Savvaty is the only tent-roof church in the monastery architectural ensemble. The tent roof is decorated with green tiles depicting warriors and guns. Two picturesque wings of the infirmary and the uprising tent-roof, crowned with a small cupola, remind of a bird and symbolize eternal memory of the heroes and victims of the Time of Troubles honoured by the contemporaries and descendants.

Another modest structure in the monastery reminds of tragic events which took place in the early 17th century. It is Boris Godunov and his family's vault, situated at the western wall of the Cathedral of the Dormition. (Originally the tombs were inside the parvis. When the parvis was dismantled in 1780, they emerged outside the cathedral and were covered with a tent.) (25). Boris Godunov, a talented politician and an experienced courtier, was elected Tsar without precedent and became one of the most outstanding and tragic figures in Russian history. Tsar Boris

Москва. MOSCOU. Троице-Сергиевская Лавра Московской губ. Le Couvent Troizy Sergei Gouvernement Moscou.

14

14. *The Trinity-St. Sergius Laura*
Late 19th century
Picture postcard

15

15. *The Cathedral of the Trinity as seen from the south*
1850s
By P. Belopolsky after P. Dilitsin's drawing (1852)
Lithographic printing-office of the Trinity-St. Sergius Laura
Black-and-white lithograph
37.5 x 51

◁ *Trinity-St. Sergius Laura, bird's eye view*

16. *Panorama of the Trinity-St. Sergius Laura*
View from the south-east

17. *Panorama*

of the Trinity-St. Sergius

Laura

View from the north-west

Godunov contributed numerous donations, including bells and unique works of art, to the Trinity Monastery. After all peripeteias of his life Boris Godunov found rest in the cloister, which he had generously favoured. His remains were transferred from the Moscow Monastery of St. Varsanofy together with the remains of his wife and son, murdered when False Dmitry I arrived. Tsar's daughter Xenia, nun Olga, died in the Suzdal Monastery and was buried in the family vault.

In the 16th and the first half of the 17th century the land property of the Trinity-St. Sergius Monastery considerably expanded. The monastery had estates practically in all parts of Russia. Land was donated, sometimes bought or changed. The unique document, recording contributions to the Monastery — *The Book of the 17th-century Donations* — mentions 600 princely, boyar and noble families — donators of the Trinity Monastery in the 16th —17th centuries. According to the Book of Donations, in the 16th century the monastery received, except lands and treasures, about 60 thousand roubles. To estimate the sum, we shall mention the fact that one could buy a village or several small villages for 30-50 roubles at that time.

The Trinity Monastery was engaged in active trade, it had its trade yards and shops in Moscow, Novgorod, Tver, Nizhny Novgorod and in other towns. There were also salt sites, fisheries and beaver hunting grounds. They said that there were three most powerful men in Moscow: Tsar, Patriarch and the Trinity Monastery Cellarer (the elder in charge of all monastery possessions). The Trinity elders were present, when the Tsar's will was written, they were invited to coronations and diplomatic receptions, they took part in the election of Tsar Mikhail Feodorovich Romanov. By the 17th century, the property and income of the Trinity-St. Sergius Monastery could be compared with those of the Tsar. In the 1640s, by the order of Tsar Mikhail Feodorovich, they composed the Inventory providing most valuable information for history investigators. The detailed description is supplemented with the unique late 17th-century icon — the earliest depiction of the Trinity Monastery (12).

18. *View of the Trinity-St. Sergius Laura from the Cellarer Pond*

19

The Greek Archdeacon and writer, Paul of Aleppo, who accompanied Makarios, Patriarch of Antioch in his visits to Russia in the 17th century, described the monastery in the following way: "It is constructed like the fortress of Damask, and its size could be compared to the town of Emess. Its high, newly built wall is as white as a dove. It is surrounded by gardens arranged in continuous concentric rings a large town…ponds and mills." Deeply impressed by the fortress walls, Paul of Aleppo exclaimed: "Mind cannot grasp their strength and beauty!"

In the last decade of the 17th century, the Trinity-St. Sergius Monastery was in the centre of political events again. In 1682, frightened with uprising Streltsi, young Tsar Peter, his brother Ivan and Tsarina Sophia took refuge behind the massive Trinity walls. Several years later, in 1689, during the second Streltsi uprising, inspired by Sophia, the monastery saved Peter again.

21

21. *Cathedral of the Trinity*

(1422)

and St. Nikon Chapel

(1548)

View from the east

When the uprising was suppressed and Streltsi's leader Feodor Shaklovity and other conspirators were executed, Peter returned to Moscow an absolute ruler of the great country. Observing the tradition, Peter gave money and works of art in gratitude for his salvation. Nevertheless, Peter's attitude towards the Trinity Monastery did not release it from the Tsar's edict, ordering the monasteries to contribute to the reforms in the army. The Trinity-St. Sergius Monastery was to provide money for the building and equipment of three ships. Several bells were taken to Moscow to be recast into cannons.

Fortunately, Tsar Peter ordered to preserve the 15th-century bell, as he was fond of antiquities himself.

The late 17th century was marked by the construction of the refectory with the Church of St. Sergius (1686-1692) and *Chertogi* Tsar's Palace. These fine buildings of impressive size (about 86 metres long) framed the central square of the monastery from the south and north.

The refectory of the Trinity-St. Sergius Monastery is one of the best specimens of the 17th century Russian architecture (29, 30), which has come down

24. *Church of the Holy Ghost (1476) and Cathedral of the Dormition (1559-1585)*

23. *Cathedral of the Trinity Interior with shrine of St. Sergius*

to us practically unchanged. Resting on a high socle, surrounded by an open gallery with semicircular arches and completed with a higher church from the east, the refectory looks like a large ship, slowly floating through the centuries. The huge size of the refectory is accentuated by the miniature Church of St. Micheas, constructed in 1734 over the tomb of St. Sergius's disciple, who, according to *The Life of St. Sergius of Radonezh*, witnessed the Appearance of the Virgin to St. Sergius. In contrast with the austere ancient cathedrals with undecorated white walls, the refectory is completely covered with polychrome ornaments. The wide windows are decorated with fine frontals with intricate stucco moulding, supported by white-stone colonnettes with relief coloured ornamentation, echoing the picturesque vine-leaf motif around the columns between the windows. Looking at these magnificent patterns and chequered painted walls, you might recall the 17th-century splendid vestments of brocade and velvet embroidered in pearls and precious stones in which the royal family and courtiers entered the spacious and lighted hall of the refectory (31). It was the largest hall with a vault without a single supporting pillar in Russia at that time (its floor-space is 510 square metres). In the 1770s, by the order of Catherine II, the interior walls and vaults of the refectory were decorated by a group of painters headed by A.N. Yankovsky. Since then, the murals have been renovated more than once. Now, there no receptions there, the refectory is used for church services. The Church of St. Sergius is not large, so people pray in the refectory hall. The iconostasis, brought in 1948 from the Moscow Church of St. Nicholas the Big Cross, perfectly harmonizes with the interior of the church. It is decorated with gilt woodcarving and silvered stucco moulding.

25. *Cathedral of the Dormition (1559-1585) and Chapel-over-the-Well (17th century)*

26. *Cathedral of the Dormition*

Interior

The upper tier of the church housed the monastery library, a major collection of manuscripts and printed books, which comprised more than 600 volumes in the mid-17th century.

The Trinity-St. Sergius Monastery was universally regarded as the first cloister in Russia. It was frequently visited by the royal family, so there had been special Tsar and Tsarina Chambers, since olden times. In the late 17th century the Tsar Palace was constructed (32). Magnificently decorated, with chequered wall paintings, like the refectory, the Tsar Palace corresponds to its fabulous name. Now, it is used as one of the buildings of Moscow theological schools, Seminary and Academy, transferred to the Trinity Monastery in the 18th–early 19th century. The small Chapel-over-the-Well (37) was built over the spring at the south-western corner of the Cathedral of the Dormition at the same time with the refectory and the Tsar Palace and, probably, by the same craftsmen. The same style of the decoration made the miniature chapel look like precious casket or reliquary. Bright and elegant, it stands out against the cathedral stressing its grandeur and size.

In the 1690s, the main entrance to the Monastery was marked by the Gate-Church of St. John the Baptist (1693-1699) (33). It was built with funds of Grigory Stroganov, a representative of the well-known family of leading Russian industrialists. It was the time, when new economic relations developed and merchants and industrialists emerged at the political stage. The families, who

27

27. *Infirmary*
(1635-1638)
and the Church
of the Virgin of Smolensk
(1745-1748)

got their titles and privileges for their contribution to the development of Russian commerce, were replacing boyars in the spheres of charity and patronage of art. And it was the new attitude of the royal court that allowed Stroganov to build the church in the "Tsar abode". Rising over the monastery gate, freely interpreting classical elements, the Church of St. John the Baptist was a kind of symbol of the new time. The new time, dictating new relations between the State and the Church, greatly changed the position of the Trinity-St. Sergius Monastery.

28. *Duck Tower*
17th century

29

29. *Refectory*
View from the east

30

The Trinity-St. Sergius Monastery in the 18th Century

In 1744, Peter the Great's daughter Empress Elizabeth Petrovna honoured the Monastery with the title of Laura. However, in 1764, in the reign of Catherine II the Trinity Monastery shared the fate of all Russian convents. Its vast lands and more than a hundred thousand peasants were proclaimed the state property. The Trinity-St. Sergius Laura was to have yearly provision, restricted number of monks and servants and small holdings of land in Posad and country residences.

The monastery got used to the new conditions rather quickly, supplementing the state provision with income of trade at the Krasnogorskaya Square, tenement houses, hotels, shops and pubs.

By the 18th century the growing villages and settlements had practically formed a town around the monastery. Its location on the road from Moscow to the northern towns and numerous pilgrims promoted crafts and trade. Apart from common craftsmen, there were icon painters and woodcarvers, who established traditions, developed by contemporary artists. In 1782, the royal edict of Catherine II ordered to arrange the settlement into the town of Sergiev Posad with a town hall and emblem. But not a single problem of the town life was settled without interference of the Trinity authorities. Thus, their relations with the town administration were rather complicated.

The Trinity-St. Sergius Laura remained a major monastery in Russia, despite all changes in administrative and economic relations with the state. The Russian Emperors regularly came on pilgrimage, gave presents, contributed to the construction of new edifices. The Trinity-St. Sergius Laura was under special patronage of the royal family. Metropolitan Platon, the confessor of Catherine II, was the Laura Father Superior. At his time the monastery architectural ensemble was completed.

Metropolitan's Residence, a house of higher clergy, acquired their present appearance. The main part of the building is composed of the 16th-17th century chambers which were reconstructed and got new facade decoration in the 18th century.

30. *Refectory (1686-1692) and the Church of St. Micheas (1734)*

31. *Refectory. Interior*

32

32. *Tsar Palace*
17th century

Baroque style, extremely popular in the 18th-century Russia, is traced in the architectural ensemble of the Trinity-St. Sergius Laura, as well. In 1745-1748, a Church, consecrated to the miraculous icon of the Virgin of Smolensk, was built with funds of Empress Elizabeth's favourite, Count Alexei Razumovsky (27). The church has a circular plan. The soft lines of two sloping staircases with a massive balustrade on elegant colonnettes encircle the blue church, like a foam wave. The same soft rhythm is repeated in the intricately-shaped roof. The Church of the Virgin of Smolensk reminds of beautiful rotundas of the 18th-century splendid park ensembles, and its miniature cupola looks like a lady's elaborate coiffure. In the 19th century the church was decorated with frescoes, in 1856 the lost iconostasis was replaced by the similar iconostasis from the Moscow Church

33. *Gate Church*
of St. John the Baptist
(1693-1699)

42

of St. Paraskeve Pyatnitsa, destroyed in Pyatnitskaya Street. This iconostasis, embellished with splendid gilt carving, is referred to the best specimens of the mid-18th century. The Royal Doors with openwork carving and relief images of the Evangelists are superb. The traditional images of Christ and the Virgin flanking the Royal Doors are cut along the contours and protruded.

The slender blue-and-white Church of the Virgin of Smolensk is in perfect harmony with a neighbouring bell tower, which was laid simultaneously, but completed twenty years later.

The grandeur and glory of Russian monasteries were often associated with the height and beauty of their bell towers.

The bell tower of the Trinity-St. Sergius Laura (1740-1770) became a symbol of its significant role in Russian history. The first project of the bell tower, designed by a court architect Johann Jacob (Ivan) Schumacher, was improved by the famous Moscow architect Ivan Michurin and completed by his pupil Dmitry Ukhtomsky, who supervised the construction (36).

The five-tier bell tower is one of the best monuments of the 18th-century Russian architecture. Its elegant shape is stressed by numerous white columns against the blue walls. The wide tier arches, decorative vases and balustrade colonnettes make it light and ethereal. At the same time, the bell tower is monumental and stable due to its massive ground tier decorated with frontals and carved white-stone cartouches with Tsar's monograms. The bell tower has an extraordinarily proud cupola shaped like a figured bowl with royal crowns. Its gold glitters brightly against the velvety blue summer sky. There chime dozens of bells, including the oldest "Nikonov Bell" (1420) and "Swan" (1594) donated by Boris Godunov (36). (Originally there were 42 bells, including the monastery "tsar bell", weighing 6,5 tons. Subsequently their number approached 50.) In 1784, by the order of Catherine II the craftsman from Tula made the first tower clock with chime, replaced in 1905 (35). In 1792, was unveiled the stone obelisk with a sun clock and four oval boards with the text reminding of the monastery's role in " preserving the Motherland". The text was written by Metropolitan Platon himself. The Laura bell tower, highest in Russia (more than 87 metres high) is a compositional centre combining the monastery edifices of different periods and styles. It became a finale in the splendid architectural "symphony" of the monastery ensemble, where each monument plays its unique part, stressing the peculiarities of the neighbouring monuments.

The 19th – early 20th century reconstruction and changes damaged the ancient ensemble. It was only the large-scale restoration of the 1940s–1960s that cleared the unique monuments of the subsequent annexes. In 1993, the monastery architectural ensemble was inscribed on the UNESCO World Heritage List.

In the course of several centuries the monastery territory turned into a real museum of architecture. Within the monastery walls there lived and worked medieval writers and philosophers, icon painters, carvers and jewellers.

34. *Chapel-over-the-Well*

17th century

37. *Bell Tower*
(1740-1770)
and the Cathedral
of the Dormition
(1559-1585)

35

35. *Bell Tower*

36. *Bells of the bell tower*

36

The monastery was a major cultural centre of Old Russia. The monasterial sacristy had accumulated priceless works of art donated by Moscow Grand Princes, Tsars and Boyars. These remarkable works of art are much older, than the Sergiev Posad State History and Art Museum, where they are preserved now, but it was here that their new life began.

The museum was established in 1920 by the Decree of the Soviet Government on the basis of the art treasures of the Trinity-St. Sergius Laura, nationalized after the 1917 revolution. Early museum's history is connected with scholars and philosophers: P.A. Florensky, Yu.A. Olsufyev, a.o. The ancient monuments were

38. *Fortress wall with*
Vodyanaya (Water) Tower
(18th century)
and Lukovaya (Onion-
shaped) Tower
(16th-17th centuries)

39. *View of the Church*
of St. Elijah (1773)
from the Cellarer Pond

40. *Churches*
of the Presentation
in the Temple and
of St. Parasceve Pyatnitsa
(16th-17th centuries)

studied, restored, displayed for everybody who is interested in Russian culture. Over the years of its existence, the museum has enriched the art collection by more than ten times. The ancient collection is logically supplemented with the collections of Russian folk and contemporary art.

You can perceive succession of many generations of artists here and correlation of two streams of Russian culture – professional and folk art. The museum offers a unique opportunity to see the monuments of different epochs. So, it is justly called a hermitage of Russian culture from the 14th till the 20th century. On the territory of the Trinity-St. Sergius Laura there has been formed a unique historical and cultural complex incorporating the functioning monastery, theological schools and the museum reserve. Each element of this complex preserves, in its way, spiritual, historic and artistic heritage and memorials of this wonderful place where Russian soul is alive.

Old Russian Art
of the 14th–17th Centuries

In the unique collection of the Sergiev Posad Museum Reserve a special place is occupied by the collection of Old Russian Art of the 14th–17th centuries. It comprises icons, a lot of masterpieces of the most celebrated painters among them; magnificent ecclesiastical and ornamental embroideries, which are, for the most part, classical specimens of Russian medieval art; splendid works of gold- and silversmiths, striking with superb skill and variety of techniques, and unique small sculptures attracting with individual manner of carving and original iconography.

A remarkable peculiarity of the collection is in the fact that it is not a set of occasional anonymous items, it had been accumulated in the Trinity-St. Sergius Laura in the course of several centuries. Each item has its history and reason for its creation and arrival. The treasures were mainly donations of Russian Tsars, Grand and Apanage Princes, boyars, clergymen merchants and servicemen. The Monastery documents mention about 600 ancient princely, boyar and noble families once closely connected with the Trinity-St. Sergius Monastery. There were different reasons for donations. Thus, the Tsars and Grand Princes marked their coronation, birth of an heir, important victories, Most often donations arrived "for keeping the soul" of dead relatives, for the right to take monastic vows and for the right to be buried on the monastery territory. The icons, brought on the coffins, passed to the Monastery, as a rule. So, every item, be it a painted image of a saint, small carved pectoral icon, monumental shroud or touching object of everyday life, is linked with history.

They remind of the important events of Russian social life and reflect the significant role, played by the Trinity-St. Sergius Monastery. The latter was connected with Moscow from the beginning. It influenced greatly the character of the collections mainly reflecting the development of Moscow art school.

But not all items in the monastery collection were donations. The Trinity-St. Sergius Monastery itself was an ancient cultural centre: there were experienced painters, jewellers, wood and bone carvers, skilful scribes in its workshops. Their names are preserved on several works that they once made. For special

41

41. *St. Anna*

with the Infant Mary

14th century. Serbia (?)

Tempera on panel, silver,

embossing, gilding;

46.5 x 37.5

works the monastery authorities often commissioned craftsmen from Grand Prince and Tsar workshops.

Thus, the donations, works of the Trinity artisans and works, commissioned by the monastery, form the basic stock of the ancient collection. Its historic and artistic significance is really great. It is just impossible to get a good idea of Moscow Rus art without it. A large number of precisely dated and signed monuments of this collection characterize certain periods and even certain kinds of art of four centuries.

The ancient collections have been carefully preserved, restored, investigated and supplemented with interesting items by the museum.

At present, they are displayed in two large expositions – *Old Russian Icon Painting* and *Old Russian Applied Art*.

42. *The Virgin Peribleptos*
14th century. Byzantium
Tempera on panel, gold,
pearls, precious stones,
embossing;
71 x 57.5

42

43. *The Virgin of the Don*

Late 14th–early 15th century. Moscow

Donated by Vasily Obedov

Tempera on panel, gold, silver, precious stones, embossing gilding; 28.5 x 21

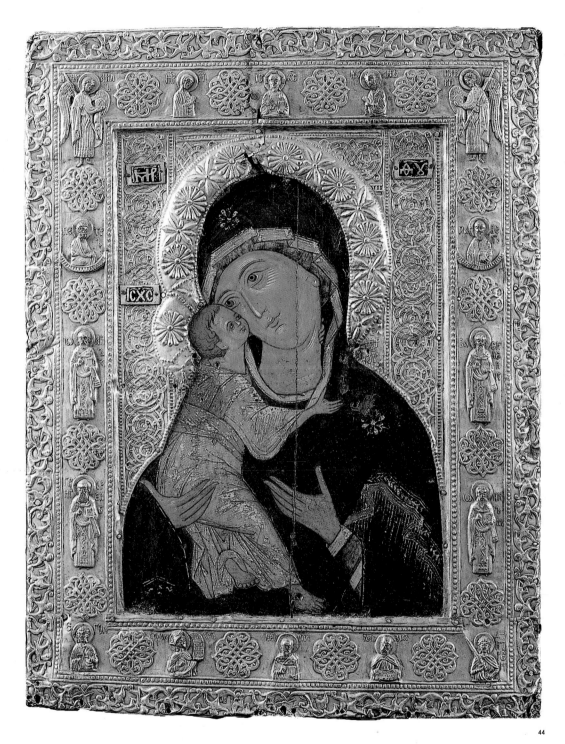

44

44. *The Virgin of Vladimir*

Late 14th—early 15th century. Moscow

Donated by Boyar Mikhail Vasilievich Obraztsov

Tempera on panel, silver, chasing, embossing, gilding; 34 x 27

46

Old Russian Icon Painting

The display Old Russian Icon Painting is housed now in six halls in the first floor of the Treasury Building. One can see here rare monuments of the 14th century, icons painted by Andrei Rublev and his disciples, various 16th-century works, early 17th-century icons by artists of the Stroganov School, works of the second half of the 17th century by Tsar's iconographer Simon Ushakov.

The icons in the Museum collection are original as far as their iconography is concerned. A significant place is occupied by small icons depicting the Virgin in the most popular variants: Hodegetria, Eleusa, the Virgin of Tikhvin, the Virgin of Kazan, and others. For the most part they were revered family icons donated by Moscow princes and boyars. Numerous representations of the Virgin vividly demonstrate the ability of Russian icon painters to express diverse feelings within the limits of the same iconographic schemes.

St. Anna with the Infant Mary attracts with rare iconography and perfect painting (41). This icon puts in mind Serbian 14th-century icons. It is connected with a godson of Superior Sergius, a Serbian nobleman, Vojeiko Voitehovic, who came to serve Moscow Prince Dmitry Donskoi in the 14th century and was buried in the Trinity Monastery. The representatives of the Vojeikovs were buried here till the early 17th century. *The Virgin Peribleptos* (42) reminds of the close connections between Moscow Rus and Byzantium. Its Constantinopolitan origin was mentioned in the early Monastery documents. It is also confirmed by the extant inscription in Greek on the icon.

55

47. *The Nativity of Christ*

Tablet icon. 15th century. Moscow

Tempera on panel;

23 x 18

48

48. *The Purification of the Virgin*

Tablet icon. 15th century

Tempera on panel;

23 x 18

49

49. *The Baptism*

Tablet icon. 15th century. Moscow

Tempera on panel;

23 x 18

50. *The Entry into Jerusalem*

Tablet icon. 15th century. Moscow

Tempera on panel;

23 x 18

51

51. *The Incredulity of St. Thomas*

Tablet icon. 15th century. Moscow

Tempera on panel;

23 x 18

52

52. *Image of Christ "Not Made by Human Hands"*

Tablet icon. 15th century. Moscow

Tempera on panel;

23 x 18

The name "Peribleptos" means "beautiful by appearance", "revered". This icon is supposed to have been painted by the Byzantine Ignatius the Greek to the order of Prince Yuri Dmitrievich of Zvenigorod, son of Dmitry Donskoi. Prince Yuri might have used this icon to bless the marriage of his elder son Vasily Kosoi with Feodosia, the daughter of Prince Andrei Vladimirovich of Radonezh. Prince Vasily had no heir and after his death the icon might have been donated to the Trinity-St. Sergius Monastery.

The most interesting group represents the late 14th – early 15th century icons, connected with Moscow Principality. They characterize one of the most remarkable period in Russian history after the battle at Kulikovo Field. Moscow art of the period incarnated the ideas of unity, fraternal love and charity. The spiritual content unites works of diverse artistic trends, created in Moscow at that time.

The Virgin of the Don (43) could have been influenced by the artistic manner of Theophanes the Greek, a famous master of expressive, emotional painting.

Many Moscow icons of the late 14th – early 15th century reveal lyrico-contemplative state and inner harmony of images. The *Virgin of Vladimir* (44) which once belonged to Moscow Boyar Mikhail Vasilievich Obraztsov, is a real masterpiece of this trend. The image of the Virgin is refined and poetical. The expressive lines and bright colour scheme underline her youth and beauty. It is one of the most famous iconographic variants of the Virgin, caressing the child, which was called "The Virgin Eleusa (of Tenderness)" in Russia. Igor Grabar interpreted such icons as an "ancient song of motherhood".

Worthy of attention is *The Old Testament Trinity* (45) which could have been painted in the Trinity-St. Sergius Monastery for one of the churches consecrated to the Trinity. The painter, reconsidering the traditional subject, which had most often been interpreted as Abraham's and Sarah's hospitality, concentrated on the Angels. They occupy nearly the whole surface of the board expressing quiet contemplation and harmony.

At the turn of the 15th century Moscow art found its most vivid expression in Andrei Rublev's art. The name of this celebrated artist is inseparably associated with the Trinity-

53

53. *The Crucifixion*

Late 15th century. Moscow

Tempera on panel, silver,

pearls, stones of little value,

embossing, gilding;

45 x 36.5

54. *The Elevation of the Cross*

16th century. Moscow

Tempera on panel;

71 x 56.5

56

55. *The Nativity of the Virgin*

16th century. The Volga Area (?)

Tempera on panel;

93,5 x 74

St. Sergius Monastery. In its highly spiritual atmosphere his world view was formed. Here, he painted his famous *Old Testament Trinity* "in praise" of Sergius of Radonezh. In the 1420s, together with Daniel Chorny he decorated the Cathedral of the Trinity with frescoes and icons. The iconostasis of the cathedral, created under the supervision and with participation of Rublev, is a unique monument of Russian art. It is one of the first samples of Russian tall, many-tiered iconostases, and a rare ensemble, which has been completely preserved. Only the Royal Doors (46) were replaced and transferred to the small church in the refectory in the 17th century. The 15th-century Royal Doors are displayed in the museum now. Their simple, yet, carefully worked out composition, rhythmical lines of expressive silhouettes, soft colours prove that they were directly influenced by Andrei Rublev, if not painted by himself. The images of the outstanding master and the artists of his circle convey the ideal features of visual and spiritual beauty of their contemporaries. They are deeply spiritual, lyrical, and warm.

Andrei Rublev's art greatly influenced the following development of Old Russian icon painting. The 15th century is the time of its brilliant heyday, the time when Rublev's heritage was creatively interpreted. The icons of the period are distinguished by calm concentration and peculiar brightness. Perfection of artistic manner, superb command of design, colour scale, composition, techniques are characteristic. Fine specimens of such art are miniature tablet icons (47-52), painted on canvas covered with gesso ground on both sides (such icons were called "towels"). Sets of such icons were painted for church services: they were put on the church lectern on days of religious feasts or when the memory of some saint was honoured. The numerous icons, displayed in the museum, prove the great talent and striving for high spirit of the 15th century icon painters.

Artistic quests of the 15th century were realized in art of Dionysius, the famous icon painter, who lived and worked at the turn of the 16th century. The works of Dionysius's circle are distinguished by solemn festivity, elegant forms, free compositions and refined colouring.

This trend can be illustrated by *The Crucifixion* (53) displayed in the museum,

65

57

which depicts the most tragic Gospel scene. It attracts first of all by light graceful figures of the interceding saints and exceptionally beautiful figure of Christ. The artist stressed admiration and worship for the feat of redemption for the mankind rather than death and suffering. Thus, the figures of the Virgin and the Holy Women behind Her are so reserved and majestic, John the Theologian is so pensive, and Longinus the Centurion is so stricken.

The artistic achievements of Dionysius and his disciples were further developed in the 16th century. Since the 16th century, icon painting of the Moscow School took the leading place in Russia.

The 16th-century icons were of high artistic level, but their content was quite different. Many of them clearly expressed political and moralistic themes, much attention was paid to complicated theological dogmas. *The New Testament Trinity* (58) is an original icon conveying the Christian dogma of the Triune God. This iconography was known in Russia since the 14th century. The idea of the Triune God constantly arouse hot religious debates. The 16th-century heretic movements made this theme urgent again.

The religious and philosophic ideas of that period were reflected in the *Nativity of the Virgin* (55, 56). The traditional scene was interpreted in a different way. This icon expressed complicated theological conceptions of the Virgin and Her role in Christian history. *The Nativity of the Virgin* is the first feast in the most revered cycle of the Twelve Feasts, that is why it is celebrated by the Church as the day of universal joy. The festive sence is conveyed by an extremely bright and fine colour scheme of the icon.

Turning to the images of Russian national saints is a characteristic feature of the 16th century icon painting. Sergius of Radonezh was the most venerated saint. The icons with his image are known since the 15th century. In 1591, Cellarer Eustathius Golovkin painted the icon *St. Sergius of Radonezh with Scenes from His Life* (57). As a model he used icon of the late 15th – early 16th century from the iconostasis of the Cathedral of the Trinity. The ideal image of the saint is depicted in the central part, and the border scenes show the concrete events of his life, which are perceived as the spiritual ascent of the saint.

58. *The New Testament Trinity*
Second half of the 16th century
Tempera on panel, silver, pearls,
filigree, gilding, embroidery;
27.5 x 23.5

58

57. *St. Sergius of Radonezh*
with Scenes from His Life
Icon painter, Eustachius Golovkin
1591. Trinity-St. Sergius Monastery
Tempera on panel, silver, precious
stones, chasing, engraving, gilding;
65 x 52.5

59. *The Appearance of the Virgin and St. Nicholas to Sexton Yurysh*

17th century

Tempera on panel;

31 x 26.5

60. *The Appearance of the Virgin to St. Sergius*

17th century

Trinity-St. Sergius Monastery

Tempera on panel, silver, embossing, gilding;

32.5 x 27.5

69

61

The 16th-century icons display growing narrative aspect, interest in surrounding world, objects of everyday life, architecture, landscapes. Large icons with many-figured compositions are typical of that time. *The Elevation of the Cross* (54) depicts the legend of the festive elevation of the Cross found by Empress Helena on Golgotha where Christ was crucified. The Holy Cross was elevated in front of St. Sophia Cathedral in Constantinople. The icon is fine and colourful. The main idea was to glorify Christianity and to rise its status. It echoed the policy of Russia incorporating different nationalities and converting them to the Christian faith. The architectural background and clothings, reminiscent of Russian forms and types, are skilfully executed.

Russian art of the 17th century is varied in themes and styles. It reflected strained spiritual life, predetermined by the dramatic events Russian people had to go through at the begin-

ning of the 17th century: dynastic crises, peasant rebellions, struggle for national liberation. The world view was slowly changing, new notions of a person's role were gradually emerging. But the new concepts made their way in art with great difficulty.

The majority of icons were painted in the traditions of the previous century. Such are *The Appearance of the Virgin to Sexton Yurysh* (59) and *The Appearance of the Virgin to St. Sergius of Radonezh* (60). They delicately combine the narrative element with certain inner expressiveness of the images.

New treatment of artistic tasks was most vividly reflected in icon painting of the Moscow school. In the second half of the 17th century the Moscow Armoury became a kind of Old Russian "art academy". It gathered the best artists of various branches. Icon painting there was supervised by Simon Ushakov, whose art determined the whole epoch in Russian art.

Ushakov, an educated and talented person, and his friend Joseph Vladimirov were also first art theoreticians. In their treatises they pointed out lofty tasks of art, explained advantage of "luminous" and "lifelike" painting compared to old dark-faced and conventional images, called artists to portray the visual beauty of man. The icons of Simon Ushakov were recognized and highly appreciated. Some of his works bear the author's signature.

In the museum collection the art of the prominent Tsar's iconographer is represented by the icons of the 1670s –1680s. Some of them were donated by Ushakov himself, others were presented by his patron Boyar Bordan Matveyevich Khitrovo or commissioned by the Trinity-St. Sergius Monastery.

St. Nikon of Radonezh, painted for the saint's tomb (62), is referred to 1675. The frontal representation and flat vestment treatment followed the old canons. But Nikon's face is painted in a new way: it is modelled by soft light surfaces on the forehead, cheeks and nose rather than by conventional highlights.

The Last Supper, painted in 1685 for monastery's Cathedral of the Dormition, gives a good idea of Simon Ushakov's art (61). The horizontal composition is original. In the space treatment the artist closely approached linear perspective. The figures of the Apostles and Christ are three-dimensional because of light annd shade modelling of their faces. Still, this icon, like other works, proves inconsistency of innovations of Simon Ushakov's art. He stuck to the traditional iconography, usual colour scheme and highlights. Nevertheless, the influence of his experience and theoretical views was really great. Simon Ushakov's art stimulated further quests and led to new, realistic painting.

62. *Simon Ushakov*

St. Nikon of Radonezh

1675. Moscow

Donated by Boyar Bogdan

Matveyevich Khitrovo, 1676

Tempera on panel;

215 x 69

62

63. *St. Sergius of Radonezh*

Pall. Detail

1420s. Moscow

Silk fabrics, coloured silks and gold thread; couchwork;

196 x 84

Applied Art of the 14th-17th Centuries

The exposition *Old Russian Applied Art* is housed in the former monastery sacristy, which was once a reliable depository of ancient icons, various precious utensils and vestments. Sumptuous ecclesiastical and ornamental embroideries, small-size sculptures and jewellery had constituted a major part of the monasterial treasury. In the course of several centuries the sacristy had turned into a sort of museum, where the value of the monuments was tested by the time. A lot of specimens are of unique historic and artistic value.

An exceptional place in the collection is occupied by the specimens produced in Moscow Principality and early Russian centralized state of the 14th – early 16th century. The ecclesiastical embroideries, often called "paintings with a needle", give a good idea of artistic life at that time. They were used as icon hangings, palls, covers for communial vessels, gonfalons, clergymen vestments skilfully embroidered in coloured silks, gold, silver, pearls, precious stones. Their themes are similar to those of icon painting. Icon painters always took part in their production. The characteristic features of the main periods of icon painting evolution were reflected in embroidery as well. However, different materials and techniques made the embroideries quite special. Russian women were wonderful embroiderers, and their role was very important. Their skill and taste determined the expressiveness and beauty of the embroidered items.

The embroideries were greatly appreciated and carefully preserved, as we often find them among the donations in the major convents. They were produced in special workshops. The needlewomen were specially trained. The workshop was usually supervised by the lady of the house — boyarinya, princess or tsarina, who was often a skilful embroiderer herself. Since the 15th century the leading

64. *The Crucifixion with the Selected Saints in the border*

Purificator. Mid-15th century

Workshops of the Moscow Kremlin

Taffeta, coloured silks, silver and gold thread, couchwork;

50.5 x 50.5

65. *The Entombment*

Shroud. Detail. Early 15th century. Moscow

Damask, linen, coloured silks, silver and gold thread; couchwork;

136 x 183

66

66. *The Miracle of the Archangel Michael in Konya*

Purificator

1501-1503. Workshops of the Moscow Kremlin

Donated by Grand Prince Ivan III

Taffeta, coloured silks, silver and gold thread, couchwork;

62 x 60

67, 68. *The Church Feasts*

and Selected Saints

Podea. Details

1499

Workshops of the Moscow

Kremlin

Donated by Grand Princess

Sophia Paleologus

Linen, brocatelle, coloured

silks, silver and gold thread,

gold lace, couchwork;

103 x 122

place was held by Moscow Grand Prince work-shops, which since the mid-16th century were called Tsarina's Chambers. It was there that many items from the Sergiev Posad Museum had been produced. The collection is regarded unique in all respects.

The earliest specimen dates back to the early 15th century. It is the most ancient Russian shroud depicting a scene of the Entombment (65). Its pictorial aspect is most important. Making elaborate couchwork in silk and gold threads, the embroiderers stressed the expressive design, which conveyed the tragic mood of the mourners. At the same time, the shroud is highly decorative. The gold cross-

es and stars filling the surface and echoing the gold vestments make it quite precious.

The 15th-century Moscow embroideries, like icons, reveal deep interest in person's inner world. The pall *St. Sergius of Radonezh* (1420s) (63), representing the founder of the monastery, can be regarded as a peculiar medieval portrait. With wonderful skill did the designer and needlewomen manage to portray both individual features of the real historic person and the dignity, self-concentration and genuine modesty that were so highly appreciated by his contemporaries. There is a convincing opinion that the designer of the pall was an artist of Andrei Rublev's circle. The pall was

69

69. *St. Nicholas*

Podea

Late 15th–early 16th century

Moscow

Taffeta, coloured silks, silver

and gold thread, couchwork;

48 x 63

70. *The Golgotha Cross*

Pall

1557

Workshops of the Moscow Kremlin

Donated by Tsar Ivan the Terrible and

his wife Tsarina Anastasia Romanovna

Satin, coloured silks, silver and gold

thread, couchwork;

183 x 72

undoubtedly inspired by individuality of Sergius who was an example of spiritual self-discipline for many generations.

The Moscow Kremlin workshops of Ivan III are represented in the collection by a number of samples. The purificator (chalice cover) depicting the *Crucifixion with Selected Saints* (64) is probably connected with the name of his first wife Maria Borisovna. This work is marked by great taste of the needlewomen who could combine coloured silks stitching with delicate silk threads of the background. Inorporating of gold threads makes it still more refined.

In 1499, the second wife of Ivan III, Sophia Paleologus, "Tsarina of Constantinople" and Grand Princess of Moscow, donated the large icon cloth *The Church Feasts with the Selected Saints* (67, 68) for *The Old Testament Trinity* by Andrei Rublev. The composition looks like an icon with border scenes: the centre-piece cross is framed with scenes of the feasts and images of the saints embroidered in the border. The icon cloth proves high professional skill of the designers and needlewomen. This precious donation marked the victory of Grand Princess Sophia and her son Vasily III in their struggle for the throne with the heirs by the first marriage of Ivan III.

The 15th — early 16th century Moscow embroideries demonstrate superb skill in combinations of gold thread and coloured silks. Yet, till the first quarter of the 16th century multicoloured silks prevailed. The purificator depicting *The Miracle of the Archangel Mikhail in Konya* (66), striking with its bright colours even now, is a splendid work of the period. Dionysius's style can be traced in the late 15th—early 16th century embroideries. The icon cloth St. Nicholas is distinguished by elegant elongated proportions and beautiful colour scheme (69).

The Moscow ideas of liberation, victory of good over evil and martial deeds were reflected in miniature sculptured works, which represent a specific kind of Old Russian sculpture. They are mainly pectoral icons, panagias and reliquaries made of different kinds of stone, wood and bone, decorated with carved images of saints. These objects of Christian cult had been widespread from ancient times and belonged to civilians as well as to clergymen. Made to individual orders by professional artisans, they always were of special significance for their owners. They were often given with

70

71. *The Entombment*

Shroud

16th century. Moscow

Damask, coloured silks, silver

and gold thread, couchwork;

103 x 55.5

the parents' blessing and were considered as certain amulets. So, they usually depict patron and local saints, the Virgin, Christ, St. Nicholas and St. George, who were worshipped as protectors from evil force, diseases, war and travel dangers.

The museum possesses unique stone icons of the 11th–14th century made by artisans of Byzantium, Georgia, Ryazan, Novgorod and Moscow (81-85). They reveal a fascinating world of medieval beliefs. The flourishing of small-size sculpture in the second half of the 15th century was connected with the Trinity Monastery carver and jeweller Ambrose. His best work is the triptych of carved wood in a filigree gold case, made in 1456 (84, 85).

Ambrose's image interpretation and many-figured composition were obviously influenced by Andrei Rublev's art.

The diverse 14th –early 16th century works of Moscow gold- and silversmiths acquaint us with their aesthetic ideas. The earliest articles of laconic shape and modest decoration corresponded to the tastes of that time (88).

In the 15th century, Moscow craftsmen manifested great skill in various techniques and decorative methods. Engraving and filigree were most popular. The display presents the specimens produced by the outstanding jewellers Ivan Fomin and Ambrose (84, 85, 89).

The works of the 16th-century jewellery art compose a large group in the collection.

80

73. *"The Queen Did
Stand"*

Altar cloth

Early 17th century. Moscow

Donated by Tsar

Boris Godunov (?)

Gold-thread velvet, pearls,

precious stones, coloured

silks, silver and gold thread;

couchwork;

105 x 94

73

74. *The Appearance of the Virgin to St. Sergius of Radonezh*

Gonfalon

1650. Workshops of the Moscow Kremlin

Donated by Tsar Alexei Mikhailovich and his wife Tsarina Marya Ilyinichna

Taffeta, coloured silks, silver and gold thread, couchwork;

94 x 91

The articles produced in the second half of the 16th century represent the time of Ivan the Terrible, when Moscow became an artistic centre of all Russia.

The magnificent embroideries were made in the workshop of Tsarinas chambers of Anastasia Romanovna, Mariya Nagaya and Irina Godunova. Many of them are characterized by delicate use of gold thread, enriching the multicoloured silks. The 1557 pall *The Golgotha Cross* (70), is connected with Anastasia Romanovna, the first wife of Ivan the Terrible. The Golgotha Cross symbolizes the Crucifixion. The mourn-

75. *The Virgin of the Don*
Podea
17th century. Moscow
Satin, coloured silks, silver and gold
thread, couchwork;
33 x 26

75

76. *The Appearance of the Virgin to St. Sergius*
Podea
16th century. Moscow
Workshops of Euphrosyne Staritskaya
Damask, coloured silks, silver and gold thread, couchwork;
64 x 59

77. *St. Nikon of Radonezh*
Pall
1633
Workshops of the Moscow Kremlin
Donated by Tsar Mikhail Romanov and his father Patriarch Filaret
Damask, pearls, precious stones, coloured silks, silver and gold thread, couchwork;
227 x 105

76

78. *St. Sergius
of Radonezh with Scenes
from His Life*
*Pall. Detail
1671. Stroganovs' workshop
Donated by Anna Ivanovna
Stroganova
Silk, pearls, precious stones,
coloured silks, silver and gold
thread, couchwork;
183 x 67*

78

79

79. *Yoke of phelonion*

Detail

16th century. Moscow

Donated by Prince Pyotr

Shchenyatev

Damask, pearls, pieces of glass,

coloured silks and gold thread,

couchwork;

31 x 44

80. *Sulok decoration for the*

bishop's staff

Detail. 1667. Moscow

Donated by Boyarinya Stefanida

Semyonovna Morozova

Satin, pearls, silvergilt plaques,

couchwork in gold thread;

186 x 38

80

ing angels, embroidered in the upper corners are very beautiful. The combination of fine textiles for the central part and border is selected with perfect taste. The pall was a cover for the shrine of one of the local saint: St. Sergius or St. Nikon.

The embroideries, produced in the boyar and princely workshops competed with the items from the Tsarina's Chambers. One of the best workshops belonged to Euphrosyne Staritskaya, a relative of Ivan the Terrible (the wife of his uncle, Apanage Prince Andrei Staritsky). The articles, embroidered under her supervision, are of highest quality (76). They demonstrate new decorative methods that only began to appear in the previous period: attempts to convey space, extensive ornamental couchwork in gold thread. The embroideries of Euphrosyne Staritskaya's workshop determined the evolution of embroidery in the second half and in the late 16th century. The original interpretation of the Entombment iconography, that could have appeared in Staritsky's workshop, was used in other princely and boyar workshops (71, 72).

The 16th century is a recognized period of gold-and-silver work's heyday. The best samples were made at the Moscow Armoury and

81. *SS. George and Nicholas*

Pectoral icon (obverse)

14th century. Moscow

Shale, silver, carving, gilding;

7.8 x 4.8

82. *SS. George and Nicholas*

Reverse

14th century. Moscow

the Trinity Monastery. You can see here nice engraving and niello, beautiful painted enamels, fine chasing. The gold diadems and crescent collars with pendants, donated by Tsar Ivan the Terrible for *The Old Testament Trinity* (90, 91) icon, manifest superb mastery. The combination of intricate chasing, filigree, festive enamel colours and precious stones, presents an example of wonderful harmony.

Silver ladles, cups, loving cups, bowls (86, 87) are interesting too. Their nice plastic shapes correspond to their function. In some cases the only embellishment of such article is an engraved and gilt inscription of various content, frequently naming its owner.

The monuments of the late 16th – early 17th century are marked by exceptional unity of style, artistic expressiveness and great skill. Many of them are associated with the name of Tsar Boris Godunov. The embroideries, like icons, are distinguished by precise design, but they are more ornamental, more skilful and more decorative. Their characteristic feature is a combination of embroidery with precious materials, pearls, gold plaques, coloured precious stones. One of the best samples produced

83. *SS. Boris and Gleb*

Pectoral icon

14th century. Murom

Shale, silver, carving, filigree, gilding;

8.2 x 5.3

at Godunov's workshop is the frontal (altar cover). Its composition, *The Queen Did Stand*, representing Christ with the Virgin and St. John the Baptist, interceding as principal protectors of people, symbolizes the prayer for the mankind (73). The jewellers of that time were especially fond of niello on gold (93-95). Their nielloed patterns and images are velvety black and linear. Niello, combined with other techniques, plays an important role in the embellishment of the mounting for *The Old Testament*

84. *The Crucifixion and*

Interceding Saints,

with the Church Feasts

on the wings

Triptych. Exterior

1456. Trinity-St. Sergius Monastery

By monk Ambrose

Wood, gold, pearls, carving,

filigree;

10.7 x 7.5

84

85. *The Crucifixion and*

Interceding Saints,

with the Church Feasts

on the wings

(when opened)

85

86. *Ladles*

15th century

Novgorod, Moscow

Once belonged to Novgorod

citizen Grigory Posakhno

and Moscow Boyar

Pyotr Pleshcheyev

Silver, engraving, gilding;

13 x 12; 15 x 12

87. *Loving cups*

16th century

Trinity-St. Sergius Monastery

Once belonged

to the Monastery Cellarer

Eustachius Golovkin

and Tsarina Marfa

Vladimirovna Staritskaya

Silver, engraving;

8 x 7.5; 6 x 8

Trinity by Andrei Rublev (95). The main portions of this mounting, made to Boris Godunov's order, were subsequently embellished with gold crescent collars (1626) and angels' chasubles (18th century).

The early 17th-century tendency for lavish decorativeness was completely realized in bright and luxurious patterns of applied art in the middle and second half of the 17th century.

The 17th-century embroidery is represented by a number of splendid samples, produced in the Tsarina Chamber and in the

89

88

88. *Censer*
1405
Trinity-St. Sergius Monastery (?)
Once belonged
to Superior Nikon
Silver, chasing, engraving,
gilding;
21 x 10.4

89. *Chalice*
1449. Moscow
By Ivan Fomin
Donated by Grand Prince
Vasily II the Dark
Gold, marble bowl, filigree,
engraving;
25.5 x 18.8

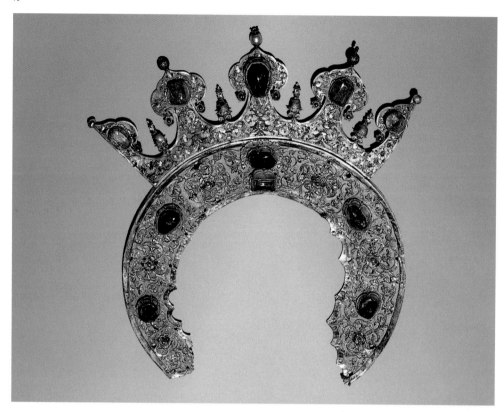

90. *Diadem*
Embellishment for the
mounting
of The Old Testament
Trinity *icon*
16th century
Workshops of the Moscow
Kremlin
Donated by Tsar
Ivan the Terrible
Gold, precious stones, pearls,
chasing;
23.7 x 29

91. *Crescent collar.*
Embellishment for the
mounting of The Old
Testament Trinity *icon*
16th century
Workshops of Moscow
Kremlin
Donated by Tsar
Ivan the Terrible
Gold, precious stones, pearls,
chasing, filigree,
granulation,
painted enamels;
30.5 x 27.5

92. *The Virgin of Kazan*

Mounted icon

16th century. Moscow

Tempera on panel; silver, precious stones, pearl-string, chasing,

gilding, painted enamels

Stroganov workshops. The royal workshops are represented by the pall *St. Nikon of Radonezh* (77) donated in 1633 by Tsar Mikhail Feodorovich and his father Patriarch Filaret Nikitich, and by the gonfalon *The Appearance of the Virgin to St. Sergius* (76) of 1650 from the workshops of Tsarina Maria Ilyinichna. The pall depicting St. Nikon (1633) demonstrates the new tastes of the period. The face is graphic and

el and precious stones. The mitre, donated in memory of Prince Feodor Ivanovich Mstislavsky, is remarkable (97). Brilliantly composed of precious plaques, studs, coloured stones, pearls, it is a genuine art treasure.

Widespread enamel perfectly corresponded to general brightness and decorativeness of the 17th century applied art. Russian craftsmen could apply enamel in different ways.

93, 94. *The Virgin and St. Mary Magdalene*

Panagia (obverse and reverse)

Late 16th—early 17th century

Workshops of Moscow Kremlin

Once belonged

to Patriarch Filaret

Gold, jasper, precious stones,

pearls, engraving, niello;

8.7 x 5.3

93   94

95. *Mounting for Andrei Rublev's icon* The Old Testament Trinity

16th—18th centuries

Workshops of Moscow Kremlin

Donated by Tsar Boris Godunov

(diadems, frame, canopy, panagia) and

Tsar Mikhail Romanov (crescent collars)

Gold, silver, precious stones, pearls,

chasing, engraving, niello,

painted enamels, gilding;

140 x 115

ornamental. The pall is extremely decorative. The gonfalon displays a delicate balance of pictorial and ornamental elements.

The pall showing St. Sergius of Radonezh (78) was donated to the Trinity-St. Sergius Monastery in 1671 by Anna Ivanovna Stroganova. It is skilfully embroidered in gold, silver, pearls and studded with coloured stones. The prevalence of gold and silver thread is a characteristic feature of the 17th century. Some embroideries look like icons mounted with precious stones (75).

The items of the 17th century jewellery are extraordinarily varied. The leading place in their embellishment belongs to chasing, enam-

Coloured enamels are used on filigree patterns of the icon mountings, chased saints and cherubs on the gold plaques decorating the mitre, donated by I.B. Repnin (96). Solvychegodsk enamels are of great interest. Their decorativeness is achieved by the combination of the dazzling white background and bright floral motifs (98).

Gold - and silversmiths of the period were fond of chasing. Chased in relief, splendid floral patterns often cover the whole surface of everyday and church utensils (99).

The 17th century was the last period in history of medieval art. In the course of its evolution Russian art had been enriched by artistic and technical achievements. Their experience gradually resulted in qualitative changes in the 18th-century art.

96. *Mitre*

1674. Moscow

Donated by Prince

Ivan Borisovich Repnin

Gold, silver, precious stones,

pearl-stringing, chasing,

painted enamels;

23 x 23

97. *Mitre*

1626

Workshops of the Moscow

Kremlin

Donated in memory of Boyar

Feodor Ivanovich Mstislavsky

Gold, precious stones, silver

thread, chasing, painted

enamels, pearl-stringing;

23 x 19

98

98. *Plate*

17th century

Silver, painted enamels;

diam.14.5; height, 3.5

99

99. *Loving cup*

17th century

Moscow

Donated by Feodor Nikitich

Apraksin in 1633

Silver, chasing, engraving,

gilding;

25.5 x 13.7

Russian Art of the 18th–19th Centuries

Metropolitans and Laura Archimandrites Platon Levshin (1737–1812) and Filaret Drozdov (1783–1867). A lot of items were made of precious materials from the sacristy to orders of the Laura authorities in the best workshops and by the leading artists of St. Petersburg and Moscow. In the course of the two centuries the monastery cathedrals, sacristy, chambers and palaces acquired items

100. *View of the reception room*

The 18th and 19th century collections are remarkable for their variety and high artistic level. For the most part, they had been concentrated in the Trinity-St. Sergius Laura. They were donations, gifts and contributions of patrons and worshippers. The sacristy was considerably completed with art treasures due to the activity of Moscow made according to the changing tastes and fashion. Among them there remained ecclesiastical, icon and ornamental embroideries in pearls and gold thread, books and church utensils of precious stones and metals. At the same time, the collection comprises nice samples of oil painting and engraving, items of glass, porcelain and faience, painted enamels, new fabrics, pieces of furniture and interior decoration.

The display presenting the works of the 18th–19th century Russian art is housed in the former Vicegerent's, built over the western part of the fortress wall between the Cellarer and Beer Towers in the middle of the 18th century. The residence was reconstructed several times, but the main reception room preserves splendid baroque stucco moulding on the ceiling. According to ancient documents, other rooms had modest interior decoration and furnishing.

Engraving was a new field of Russian culture in the 18th century. The collection of the 17th –19th century prints and lithographs is not large. It is represented by different genres. Since the second half of the 17th century woodcuts or copper engravings had played an important role in church life. Printed illustrations and head-pieces decorated books; corporals on paper or fabric depicting scenes of the Entombment were a necessary element of any church. Educational prints were widespread. Yet, portraits, landscapes, illustrations and reproductions were main genres of engraving. Printed theses and conclusions, portraits and views of towns and monasteries were interior decorations of the Laura, dwellings. The Trinity-St. Sergius Laura cooperated with artists in this field as well. In the first three decades of the 18th century it commissioned two famous engravers – brothers Ivan (1677–1744) and Alexei (1682–1751) Zubov. The printed portraits of Tsars, albums with views of the new and old capital, vedutes were donated in token of great respect to St. Sergius abode. Grand Princes Alexander and Konstantin (101) presented their portraits in the technique of stipple engraving after the drawings by Gavrila Skorodumov (1755-1792) to their confessor Archbishop Platon Levshin. The portrait of Peter I (1672–1725) by Johann Friedrich Schreyer (1768–1795) was presented to Platon by Prince A.M. Beloselsky-Belozersky together with the portraits of Russian individuals commissioned by this famous Russian envoy in the 1780s. Among various representations of Metropolitan Platon Levshin the 1803 portrait, engraved by Ignaz Sebastian Klauber (1754–1817) is distinguished by careful realistic treatment.

Portraiture was the greatest achievement of the 18th- and 19th-century Russian art. It reflected searching of a person's role in the surrounding world, attention to an in-dividuality, new conception of aesthetic, social and moral value of man and his inner world. By the mid-18th century two small portrait galleries had been collected in the Tsar (Chertogi) Palace and Archimandrite Residence. They demonstrated new tendencies in Russian social life that were unusual for church organizations, yet proved not alien to the activity of the major monastery in the vicinity of Moscow. The

101

reception room in the Vicegerent Residence was decorated with portraits in the second half of the 18th century. Both galleries incorporated of portraits of Russian Tsars and Laura Archimandrites. The portrait of Tsarina Praskovia Feodorovna Saltykova (102), ascribed to the famous painter of the first three decades of the 18th century, Ivan Nikitin (c. 1680 – c. 1742),

101. *Gavrila Skorodumov*
Portrait of Grand Prince
Konstantin Pavlovich
1787
Gift of Grand Prince
Konstantin Pavlovich
to Metropolitan
Platon Levshin
Stipple engraving;
20.7 x 18.8 (visible area)

is referred to the time of Peter I. This canvas was kept in the gallery of the Archimandrite Residence. The semi-formal portrait in calm brown colours conveys a reserved and proud character.

For many decades a leading Russian painter of the 18th century Alexei Petrovich Antropov (1716–1795) was connected with the Trinity abode and its monks. Between 1744 and 1751

ing Russia in political and church spheres. The portrait of Empress Elizabeth Petrovna (1709–1761) is an early work of the artist, the large full-length coronation portrait by Louis Caravaque being used as its model. The portrait by the Russian artist is distinguished by the more decorative colour scheme, conveying the representative and beautiful image (103).

In the mid-18th century the portraits of

102. *Ivan Nikitin*
Portrait of Tsarina Praskovya
Feodorovna Saltykova.
Before 1716
Oil on canvas;
97 x 78

102

he painted the portrait of Empress Elizabeth Petrovna commissioned by the Synod for the Tsar Palace. In 1762 he painted for the Laura the coronation portraits of Peter III and Catherine II. In the 1770s–1780s he portrayed Archimandrite of the Trinity Monastery, Moscow Metropolitan Platon Levshin, depicting an impressive social character, which corresponded to the ideas of the artist and the society of the inner world of the personality serv-

the royal couple – future Emperor Pyotr III (105) and Catherine II (104) – were painted in beautiful rocaille colouring, reflecting delicate refined characters. They were ordered for the Archimandrite Residence.

Works of applied arts constitute a significant part of the collection. In the 18th and 19th century the gold- and silversmiths and embroiderers in gold, silks and pearls developed the medieval traditions, producing specimens up

103. *Alexei Antropov*

Portrait of Empress Elizabeth Petrovna

Between 1744 and 1751

Oil on canvas; 141 x 111

104. *Unknown painter*

Portrait of Grand Princess Catherine Alexeyevna

Mid-18th century

Oil on canvas; 136 x 104

105. *Unknown painter*

Portrait of Grand Prince Pyotr Feodorovich

Mid-18th century

Oil on canvas; 116 x 97

to standards and principles of the changing artistic trends.

The works of the 18th–19th century jewellery, in which gold- and silversmiths used different techniques, are quite diverse. Through the whole period chasing remained the most traditional decoration of the book covers, icon mountings, liturgical vessels and tableware. The elaborate floral cartouches in high relief with reverse. Bright painted enamels on the gilt cover are very colourful. The cover was made by a silversmith and enameller of the Trinity-St. Sergius Laura. Enamelled plaques by the same craftsman are included in the ornamental system of the mid-18th century mitre, the cycle of Christ's Passion (120), in the gold cross (110) and in the precious panagia (111) with enamelled plaques, depicting the

106

107

106, 107. *Gospel cover*

(obverse and reverse)

1754

Trinity-St. Sergius Laura

Silver; chasing, gilding,

painted enamels;

69 x 46

figures of Christ and the Evangelists and combination of white silver and gilt details make the early 18th-century cover for the 1681 Gospel rather fanciful. The 1754 gilt cover for the large Gospel of 1689 (106, 107) is extremely complicated. It is embellished with numerous chased cartouches in baroque style which include enamel plaques depicting the Trinity, the Evangelists and scenes of the Passion on the obverse and the Tree of Jesse on the Crucifixion mounted in precious stones.

A number of magnificent works of art are connected with the names of the well-known Moscow and St. Petersburg silversmiths: G.I. Serebrennikov, P.T. Vorobei, K.I. Elers, A.I. Ratkov. Their works are characterized by intricate baroque or more balanced ornamental compositions, combination of git and white silver, elaborate chasing, fine niello. In 1787, a leading Moscow jeweller A.I. Ratkov made the incense-box of complicated shape, decorated with nielloed emblems of Russian towns (109).

The vessels of precious materials were adorned with materials that were rare in Russia, like seashells, plaques of tortoise-shell, coconut shell. In 1795, coconut shell with carved portraits of Emperor Peter I, Elizabeth Petrovna and Catherine II was included in the modest silver setting of the goblet with a chased symbol of Russia – two-headed eagle –

108. *Cover for Pontifical*

Service Book

Second half 18th century

Moscow (?)

Donated by Moscow Metropolitan

Platon Levshin, 1798

Silver; filigree, granulation, gilding;

15.3 x 10

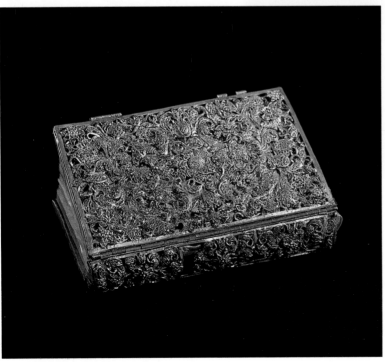

109

109. *Incense box*

1787

Moscow

By Alexei Ratkov

Gift of Catherine II

to Metropolitan Platon Levshin

for his fiftieth birthday, 1787

Silver; chasing, gilding, niello,

casting, engraving, pouncing;

21.5 x 13 x 13

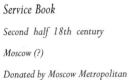

108

105

on the lid. Enamel plaques, combined with precious and imitation stones were traditional decoration of silver church vessels. They were used on the bowls and bases of the gilt chalices with relief and openwork chasing, and sculptural casting of 1788 (112) and 1832 (113), donated by A.V. Sheremetev and the wife of a Moscow priest A.M. Alexeyeva, respectively.

Fine filigree, often combined with granu-

really unique. At the early Pet-rine period, in the late 17th century, splendid shoulder-pieces were produced for the phelonions and sticharions, made in the 1730s of Empress Anna Ioannovna's and her sisters' ceremonial dresses and donated to the Trinity Monastery after the coronation. The pearlstrings, completely covering sprouts, leaves, buds, flowers, crowns and crosses, and precious stones in gilt silver

111. *The Crucifixion.* Panagia

Mid-18th century. Trinity-St. Sergius Laura

Donated by Archimandrite of the Trinity-St. Sergius Laura

Arseny Mogilyansky, 1752

Silver, gold, precious stones; chasing, cutting,

painted enamels; 8.6 x 3.4

110

110. *The Crucifixion*

Pectoral cross

Mid-18th century

Trinity-St. Sergius Laura

Silver, gold, precious stones;

chasing, gilding, cutting,

painted enamels;

16 x 11

lation, makes the articles elegant. The small Pontifical Service Book (108), donated by Metropolitan Platon in 1789, is covered with a light filigree cover. Raised intertwining silver sprouts and flowers shine softly against the smooth gilt plaques.

The 18th-century pearl and ecclesiastical embroideries in the applied art collections are

mounts or outlined in pearls, shine iridescently, creating fantastic ornamental compositions against dark-coloured velvet backgrounds. The ornamental composition on the yoke of the phelonion, donated to the Trinity-St. Sergius Monastery in 1700 by M.M. and S.A. Sheins (116), is soft and elegant. In 1757–1759, and in 1767–1771, the St. Petersburg royal work-are embroidered in pearls of different size. Combined with silver spangles, they create a magnificent baroque composition of intertwining sprouts, shells, leaves, and cornucopias. The sakkos of crimson velvet (117), embroidered in Laura's pearls by a court needlewoman Darya Likhnovskaya in 1770–1771, once belonged to the vestments kept the "pearl sacristy" of 1767-1771, made

112

112. *Chalice*

1788. Moscow. By E.P. Kuzov

Donated by Count A. Sheremetev, 1789

Silver, pieces of glass; chasing, engraving, gilding, pouncing,

cutting, painted enamels;

37.5 x 15.5

shop made for the Laura the sets of clergy vestments of brocade, silk brocade and velvet, decorated with the Laura's own pearls. The phelonion of soft-coloured brocade with the turquoise-blue yoke belongs to the set of two chasubles and sticharion (114, 115). The patterns with a Latin monogram of the Trinity-St. Sergius Laura, TSL, in the central cartouche

113. *Chalice*

1832. Moscow

By E.A. Antipiev and

monogrammist M.O.

Donated by Alexandra Matveyevna

Alexeyeva, wife of a Moscow priest

1835

Silver, turquoise, amethysts, pieces

of glass; chasing, gilding,

engraving, pouncing, painted

enamels, cutting;

34 x 18.7 x 12.3

113

114, 115. *Phelonion*

and sticharion

(right above; detail)

Mid-18th century

(before 1757)

St. Petersburg (?),

Royal Workshops (?)

Brocade, velvet, silver

spangles, gold lace and

braid; pearl-stringing,

plaiting; lengths,

phelonion 139;

sticharion 153

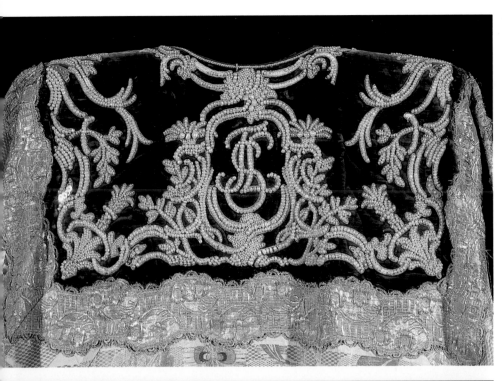

116. *Phelonion*
Detail
1700. Moscow
Donated by
M.M. and S.A. Shein in
memory of Boyar Alexei
Semyonovich, 1700
Brocade, velvet, damask,
precious stones, gold lace;
pearl-stringing, cutting;
length 153

116

by the order of Catherine II to measure of Archimandrite Platon Levshin. The whole surface of the velvet vestment is covered with intricate patterns, bouquets and vines worked in gold and silver thread, spangles and pearls of different size.

The 18th-century pearl embroidery collection was adequately completed by the frontal *The Golgotha Cross* for the communion table in the Cathedral of the Trinity (118, 119). The frontal of silk brocade is embroidered in pearls and studded with gold panagias, plaques with the 17th–18th century images in niello and enamel, numerous sapphires, rubies, emeralds, diamonds and other precious stones. It was produced in 1794–1795 to the order of Metropolitan Platon by two needlewomen – Natalya Yegorovna Baskakova, who lived in Sergiev Posad, and Praskovya Yakovlevna Shatilova, a novice of the Intercession Monastery in Khotkovo. In 1798, the latter embroidered the shroud with a scene of the Entombment in coloured silks and gold and

117. *Sakkos*

1770-1771

St. Petersburg

Royal Workshops

By Darya Likhnovskaya

Velvet, gold thread;

embroidery, pearl-stringing;

length 132

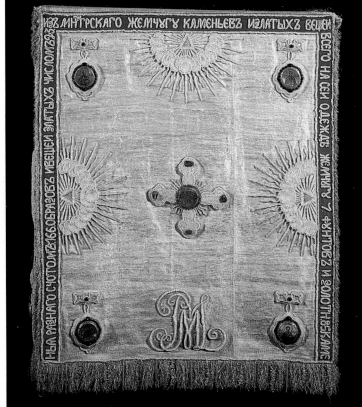

119

118, 119. *"The Golgotha Cross"*

Altar cloth

1794-1795

Trinity-St. Sergius Laura

After Ignaty Basov's drawing

By N.E. Baskakova and

P.Ya. Shatilova

Commissioned by Metropolitan

Platon Levshin

Silk brocade, pearls, precious

stones, gold, silver, gold thread

coloured silks, fringe;

pearl-stringing, cutting,

embroidery, painted enamels,

niello, chasing;

105 x 85 x 93

silver threads on the dark violet background decorated with pearls, diamonds and rubies (122). The tragic scene includes the figure of praying Metropolitan Platon.

In the 18th and 19th centuries new kinds of artistic production appeared and the royal industries of the 17th century became widespread. Glass industry had made great progress since a great number of private works, like Nemchinovs, Bakhmetiev, Orlovs and Maltsovs Factories, and the Imperial Glass Factory were opened, new techniques were used, new recipes of coloured glass developed, cut-glass was produced. Various glass articles were interior decorations and objects of everyday life, so they changed, following the style tendencies. They were decorated with engraving and with different manners of gilding. Engraving was the most common technique in glass decoration. Together with famous diamond-cutting they often used broad cutting covering the whole surface. Trailed decorations covering glasses, wine glasses and goblets is very com-

120

120. *Mitre*

Mid-18th century

Trinity-St. Sergius Laura

Velvet, precious stones, silver,

gold thread; embroidery,

pearl-stringing, chasing,

carving, gilding, cutting,

painted enamels;

22 x 23

121. *Mitre*

Second half 16th century

—1868

Moscow and the Trinity-

St. Sergius Laura

Velvet, gold, silver, precious

stones, gold thread,

and braid; embroidery,

pearl-stringing, chasing,

niello, engraving,

painted enamels, cutting;

23 x 24

121

122

122. *The Entombment*

Shroud

1798. Trinity-St. Sergius Laura

After Ignaty Basov's drawing

By P.Ya. Shatilova

Commissioned by Metropolitan

Platon Levshin

Velvet, precious stones, gold thread,

coloured silks, fringe, gold,

silver; embroidery, pearl-stringing,

cutting, gilding, painted enamels;

200 x 147

plicated (123). Craftsmen often combined different techniques in one object, comparing transparent and coloured glass with gold and silver ornaments and bronze constructive details of elaborate vessels.

In the early 18th century new kinds of ceramics were developed in Russia. Porcelain was most important. In 1747 the Imperial Porcelain Factory was opened in St. Petersburg. In 1763 in Verbilki near Dmitrov the famous Gardner Factory was founded. In the 19th century in Moscow Area and near the northern capital there were a lot of small and large works, such as the factories of Popov (124), Safronov, Kornilov, Kuznetsovs, Fediashin. The museum has collected varied items of porcelain, faience and majolica, reflecting different achievements, tastes and preferences from the late 18th till early 20th century.

At the end of the 18th century, Oriental shawls of thin wool with intricate woven patterns were in fashion in Europe. This fashion

123. *Tumblers, wine glass and goblet*

First half of the 19th century

Bakhmetiev and Maltsovs Factories

Glass, cut glass, trailed decoration, gilding, painting, etchinng; glasses, 9 x 8 and 10 x 7; goblet, 9 x 8; wine glass, 11 x 6

124. *Items from tea set:*

teapot, creamer, cup and

saucer, platter

Mid-19th century

A.G. Popov Factory.

Dmitrov District,

Village of Gorbunovo

Porcelain; printing,

overglaze painting;

teapot, 10 x 22,

creamer, 10 x 12,

cup, 10.5 x 9,

saucer, 2 x 13.5,

plate, 4 x 25.5

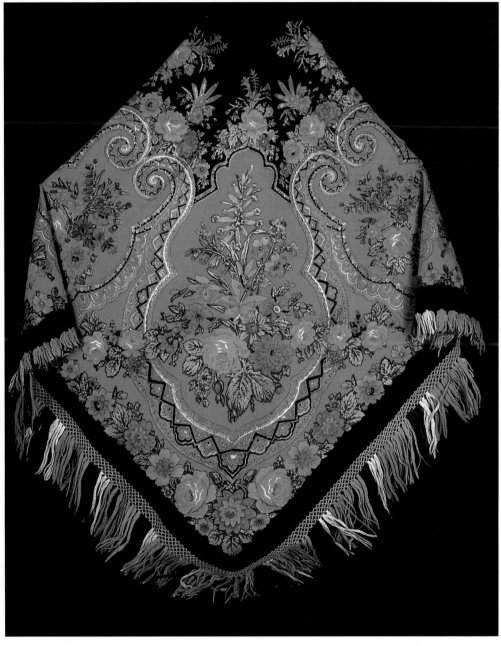

125

125. *Shawl*

Late 19th century

Moscow Gubernia

Pavlov Posad

Ya. Labzin Factory

Wool, printing;

152 x 146

was introduced in Russia as well. At the beginning of the 19th century the Merlina and Kolokoltsov Factories in Nizhny Novgorod produced elaborate double-sided shawls, kerchiefs and scarves. In the middle of the 19th century this complicated technique was replaced by printing, which promoted thin woollen shawls with coloured printed patterns.

The shawls and kerchief, produced by the Moscow Region factories were remarkable for the variety of Oriental and Russian patterns (125).

The collections of the 18th – early 20th century Russian art give an idea of the fine and decorative arts, of vivid images and perfect mastery of artists both in leading centres and provinces.

Russian Folk Art of the 18th–19th Centuries

of the Folk Handicrafts Museum (established in 1939 on the basis of the 1937 exhibition of folk art organized in Moscow's State Tretyakov Gallery) subsequently passed to the Sergiev Posad Museum, laying the foundation for the Folk Art Department. Yet, the main part of the collection was acquired by the museum expeditions organized to different regions of Russia in the 1950s–1990s.

126. *Portion of the display*

Alongside the ancient collections, presenting professional art of the 14th – early 20th century, the comprehensive collection of Russian folk art, mainly peasant art of the 18th – early 20th century, is of great significance. Folk art is displayed in the second floor of the Treasury House. The collections of the Local History Museum (established in 1926) and

The folk art collection comprises house carving from the Middle Volga Area, wooden sculpture, objects of everyday peasant life decorated with carving and ornamental painting, pottery, weaving, embroidery and printed textiles.

Folk art is interesting and original for its content. It has preserved the pictorial motifs and images of the ancient Slavonic culture. In time their meaning was forgotten. So, they were perceived like beautiful patterns included in intricate ornamentation.

Everyday peasant life bore an imprint of genuine creativity. Special attention was paid to house decoration. In the Volga Area the pediments, window cases, gates and wickets are covered with splendid relief carving. Its floral patterns are combined with the images of fab-

127. *Beer ladle*

Early 19th century

Tver Gubernia

Wood, carving;

22 x 32

127

129

128

128. *Platband of dormer*
19th century
Nizhny Novgorod Gubernia
Wood, carving;
180 x 125

129. *Casket*
19th century. Russia
Wood, metal, forging;
27 x 22.5

ulous creatures. The display presents a rich collection of such carvings (126, 128).

The museum rooms displays a lot of objects of everyday peasant life —ladles, salt-cellars, distaffs, sledges, cradles. They are made of wood and decorated with carving and painted ornaments (127, 137). They present a variety of shapes, ornaments and techniques.

117

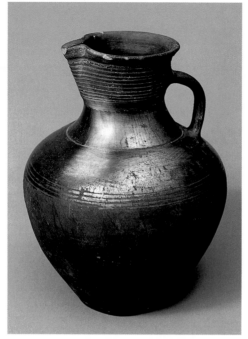

130. *Beer jug*

18th century

Moscow Gubernia

Polished earthenware;

31 x 25

131. *Jug*

Mid-19th century

Moscow Gubernia

Clay; 36 x 24

130

131

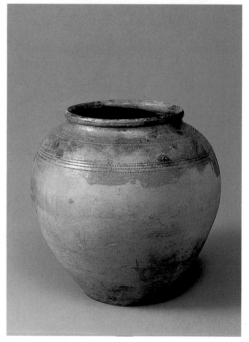

132

The objects attract by their laconic shapes and fine silhouettes. They look fantastic, reflecting folk ideas of beauty.

The collection of distaffs from different regions of Russia is unique. The variety of their shapes and decoration vividly demonstrates creative fantasy of Russian craftsmen.

Russian pottery is extraordinarily interesting. A great variety of earthenware vessels carries off a viewer by their laconic and expressive shape, beautiful texture and unity of utilitarian and artistic characteristics (130 – 133). Especially elegant is black-polished ceramics produced in numerous potteries in and around Moscow.

The ancient works of folk art displayed are samples of metalwork (129). They are forged articles decorated with openwork and stamped patterns, testifying to the old traditions of forgery. Metal plaques with diverse motifs were often used for popular chest decoration. The

132. *Korchaga jar*

Second half 19th century

Moscow Gubernia

Clay, glazing; 36 x 24

133. *Pitchers and thurible*

Second half 19th century

Moscow Gubernia

Clay, glazing;

26 x 17.5; 26 x 15; 14.5 x 9.5

134. *Wedding towel edging*

1899

Novgorod Gubernia.

Linen, cotton thread, embroidery,

weaving;

16.5 x 35

134

135

135. *Towel*

Detail

1890s.

Tver Gubernia

Linen, cotton thread,

embroidery, weaving;

242 x 35

136. *Towel*

Late 19th–early 20th century.

Tula Gubernia

Linen, cotton thread, wool,

embroidery, weaving;

364 x 35

136

combination of different techniques and various shades of colour, produces the impression of precious metal.

The 18th – 19th century weaving and embroidery are represented by the items from nearly all regions of Northern and Middle Russia. Woven and embroidered ornaments decorate clothes, head-dresses, household objects –towels, table-cloths, bed valances, etc. (134 – 136). Like carved and painted ornaments, they carefully preserved the pagan motifs (circles, lozenges, crosses, sacred deer, geese and ducks). The female figures personifying the Goddess of Earth and Fertility, and the Tree of Life flanked by sacred animals, were often used. Widespread practically in every region of Russia, they are original due to the local interpretation and variety of techniques.

Skilful weaving and embroidery were universally used for beautiful festive and wedding female garments (male costumes have not sur-

137. *Distaffs*

19th century. Arkhangelsk Gubernia

Wood, painting; heights, 92; 90

121

138

139

140

vived). Russian clothes are distinguished by characteristic cut and traditional articles (shift and *ponyova* petticoat with front opening in central areas, and shift with sarafan in Northern Russia). The costumes are very attractive due to decorative combination of two colours: white (undyed linen) and red (ornamental stripes of weaving and embroidery). These two colours suit the festive atmosphere perfectly.

Fine head-dresses — *kokoshniks, povoiniks, sorokas,* kerchiefs and shawls, embroidered in gold thread, seed pearls, beads and spangles — completed the female costumes. They are richly represented in the collection.

On the whole, the museum collection of folk art proves the great talent of Russian craftsmen who could preserve distinctly original national culture.

Contemporary Applied and Decorative Art

Many handicrafts, represented in the collection, appeared as early as the 18th–19th century. Production of toys of wood and clay is an ancient craft. Many villages and small towns of Moscow, Nizhny Novgorod, Kirov, Arkhangelsk and Tula Region are its major centres. Modern folk toys, following the best old traditions (laconic shapes, fine silhouettes, careful material treatment), attract with new brilliant image

141. *Portion of the display*

The best traditions of folk art developed in contemporary applied and decorative art. The museum collection of applied and decorative art, started with the exhibits of the Folk Handicrafts Museum, had been formed by the mid-1960s. It comprises the works of the leading handicrafts (toys, carving in wood, bone and stone, metalwork, ornamental painting on wood, miniature lacquer painting, lace-making and embroidery) and artistic industries (glass, ceramics, textiles). The display, housed in the second floor of the Treasury House, presents the best items of this collection.

interpretation. Bogorodskoye wood-carved toys (Sergiev Posad District, Moscow Region) are world-famous(143). Clay toys of Dymkovo (Kirov Region) with their archaic forms and bright colouring are famous as well (144).

Wood remains a favourite material among the masters of applied art. Carvers of Nizhny Novgorod Region follow ancient traditions. Their production, called "Khokhloma", strikes with festive golden and cinnabar painted ornaments (142).

Among the folk handicrafts, concentrated in the collection, an important place is occupied by production of different centres of miniature lacquer painting on papier-mâché. You can see here works of Fedoskino (Moscow Region) – the oldest centre that appeared at the turn of the 19th century – and younger centres – Palekh, Kholui (Ivanovo Region) and Mstyora (Vladimir Region). Fine miniatures on various boxes, brooches, decorative panels are painted in oil (Fedoskino) or tempera (Palekh, Kholui, Mstyora). Palekh painted lacquerwork is espe-

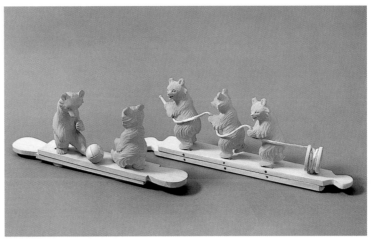

142. *O.P. Lushina*

Herbs. Loving cup

1983. Kovernino, Nizhny Novgorod Region

Lathe-turned wood, painting; 16.5 x 30

143. *N.N. Balayev*

Football players

1963

Village of Bogorodskoye, Moscow Region

Wood, carving; 26 x 10.6

V.S. Shishkin

Firemen

1967

Village of Bogorodskoye, Moscow Region

Wood, carving; 31 x 11

cially fine and precious (147, 148).

Metal trays with splendid bouquets, painted in oil upon a black or coloured background, come from the village of Zhostovo (Moscow Region) – a well-known centre of lacquer painting on metal. The collection of trays demonstrates new quests in composition, colour scheme and ornaments, and testifies to revival of the ancient techniques of painting (145, 146).

The ancient traditions of lacework are preserved in its old centres – Vologda, Yelets (Orel Region), Sovietsk (Ryazan Region), Kirishi (Leningrad Region). Each centre is character-

144. *N.P. Poroshina*

Old Man Playing Balalaika.

1964

The Musicians. 1964

L.S. Falaleyeva

Evening Meeting. 1960s

Drinking Tea. 1971

Village of Dymkovo, Kirov Region

Clay, painting;

heights, 10.5, 9.3, 14, 22

145

145. *B.F. Grafov*

Sunny Day. Tray

1985

Zhostovo, Moscow Region

Metal, oil, lacquer, painting;

47.5 x 50.5

146. *N.N. Goncharova*

Festive. Tray

1977

Zhostovo, Moscow Region

Metal, oil, lacquer, painting;

58 x 46

147

148

ized by original technique and artistic manner. Lace makers produce with great skill both miniature items and monumental decorative panels (149).

The display presents practically all kinds of contemporary applied and decorative art. One can also see here jewellery made of different decorative materials, specimens of carving in bone and stone, and fine embroideries.

An important place in the display is held by the works of leading glass works (Gus Khrustalny Glass Factory, Dyatkovo Glass Factory, St. Petersburg Art Glassworks, etc.)

146

147. *I.I. Golikov*

Three Musicians. Snuff-box

1926

Palekh, Ivanovo Region

Papier-mâché, tempera,

lacquer, painting;

11 x 7.5

148. *B.M.Yermolayev*

Dull Day Till Evening

Casket

1980.

Palekh, Ivanovo Region

Papier-mâché, tempera,

lacquer, painting;

12 x 12

149

149. *Z.A.Varaksina*

People's Friendship. Panel

Detail

1967

Sovietsk, Kirov Region.

Cotton thread, lacework;

194 x 204

150

150. *D.A. Belov*

Revival. Kerchief

Detail. 1988

Gorodets, Nizhny Novgorod

Wool, gold thread, spangles, embroidery;

173 x 156

and porcelain works (Lomonosov Porcelain Factory, Dulyovo Porcelain Factory, Dmitrov Porcelain Factory, etc.).

The content and quality of the collection demonstrate profound continuity and creative development of the ancient traditions in contemporary applied and decorative art. The above items together with the specimens of Russian folk art supplement the ancient collection, making the Sergiev Posad Museum Reserve extremely integral and offering an opportunity to see the evolution of Russian art from the 14th century till the present day.

Sergiev Posad

Art-Rodnik, Moscow, 1997